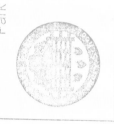

G000149603

Cat
in a
Cap

by Tim Little
Illustrated by Bill Ledger

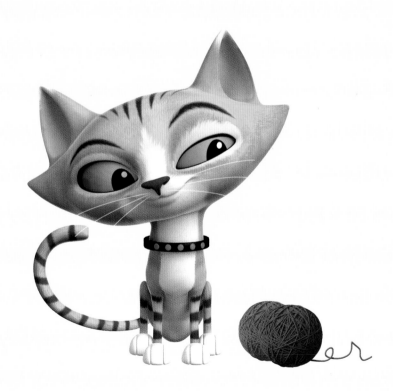

OXFORD
UNIVERSITY PRESS

In this story ...

Pip

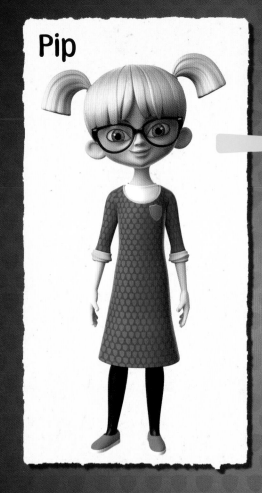

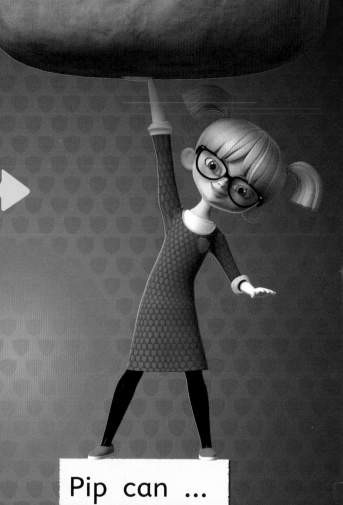

Pip can ...

Slink

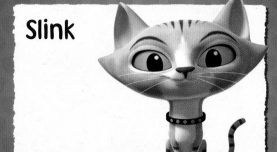

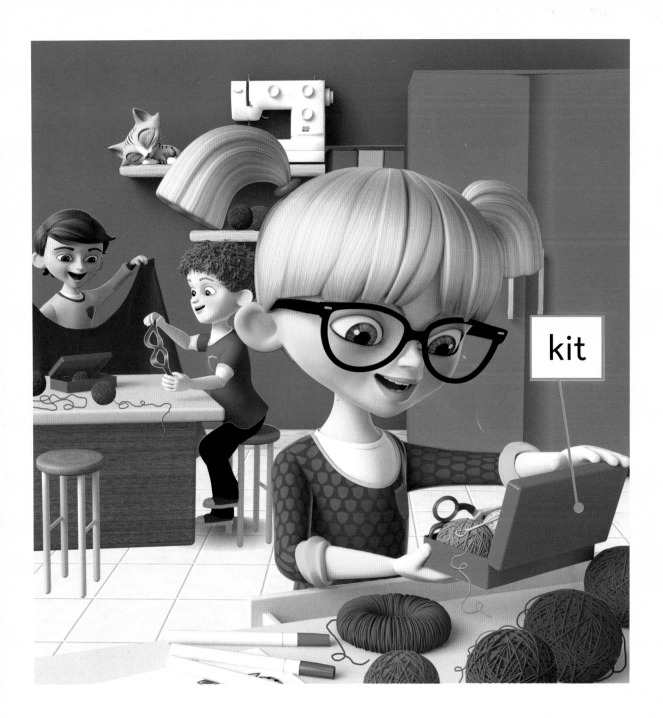

Pip got a kit.

Slink

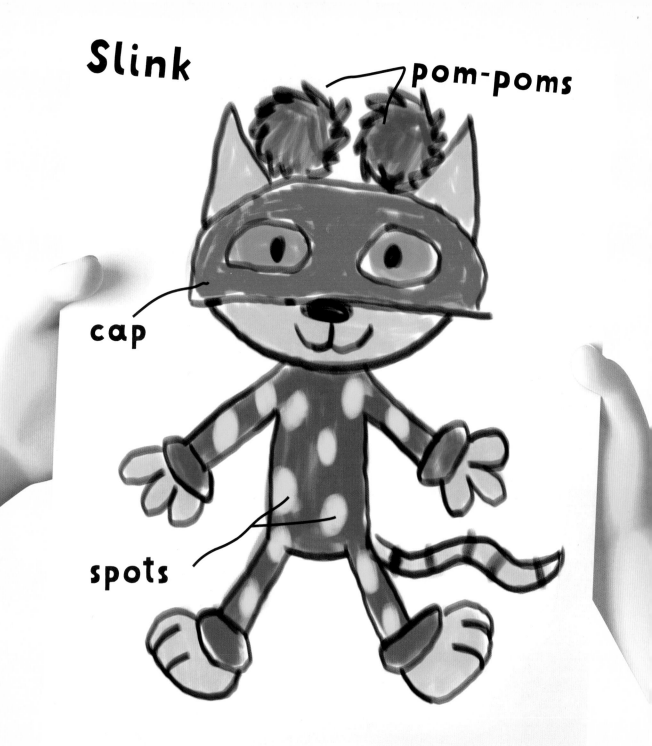

pom-poms

cap

spots

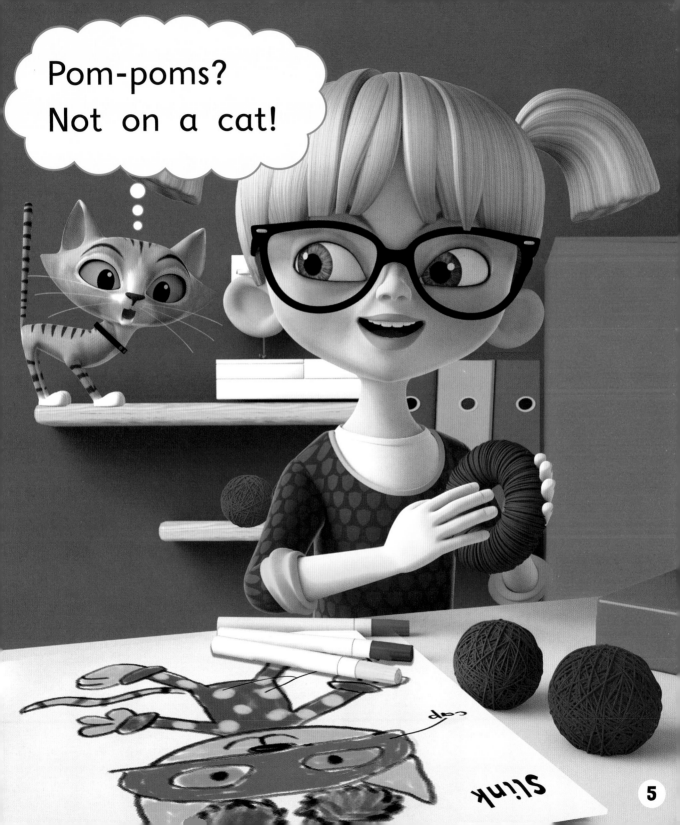

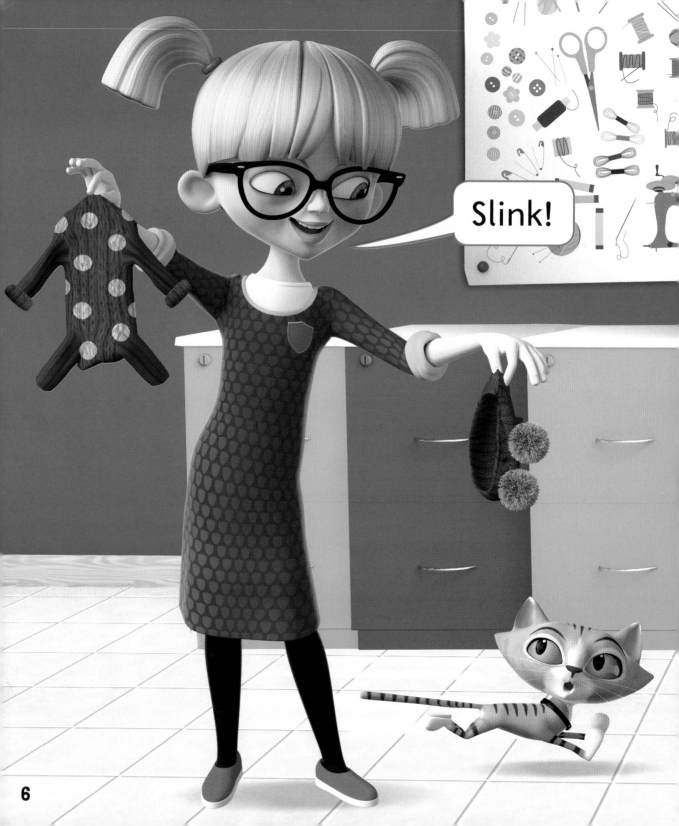

Slink!

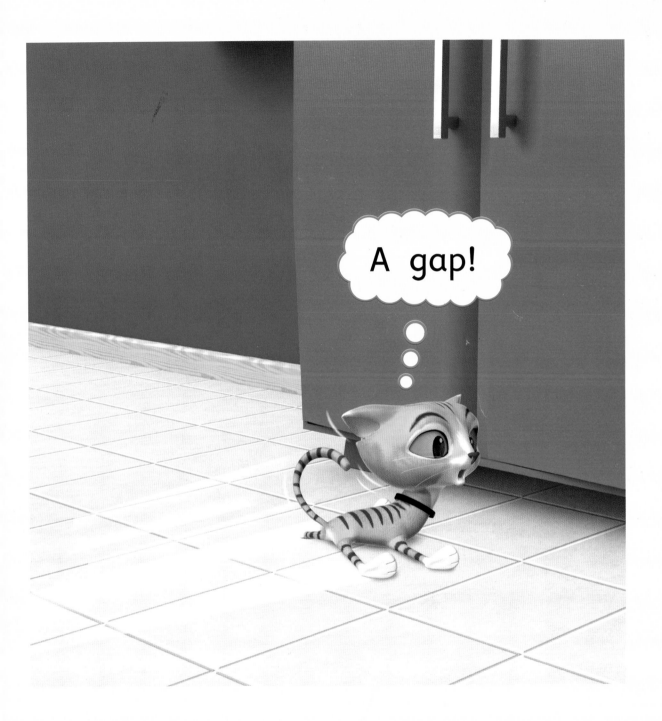

Slink skids.

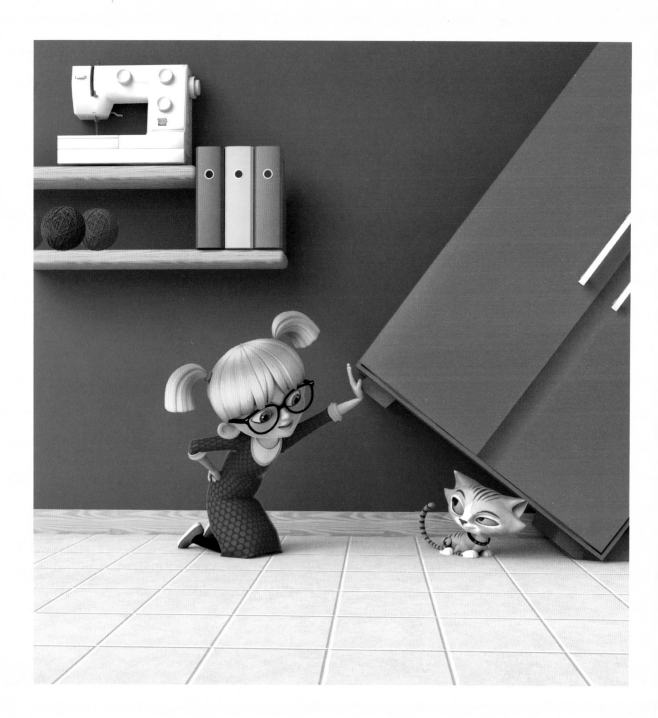

Pip can tip it.

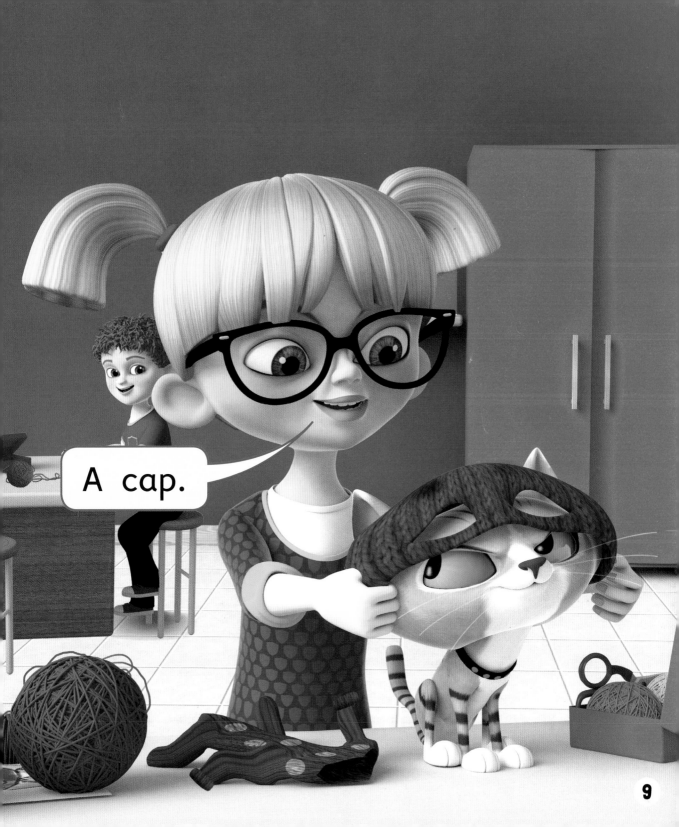

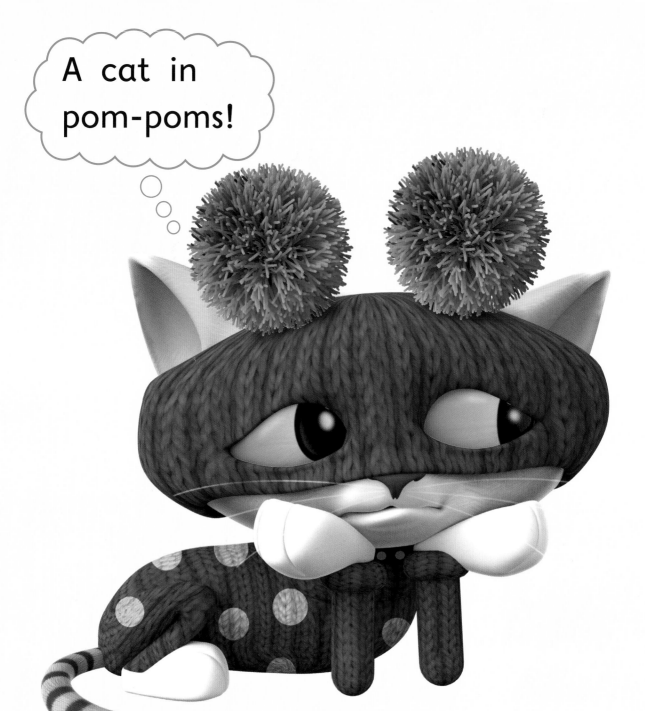

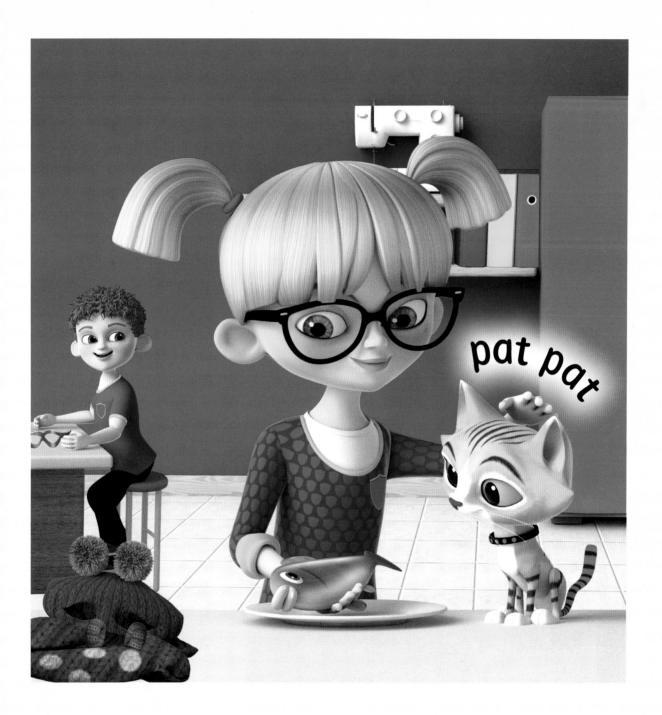

Slink got a cod.

Retell the story ...

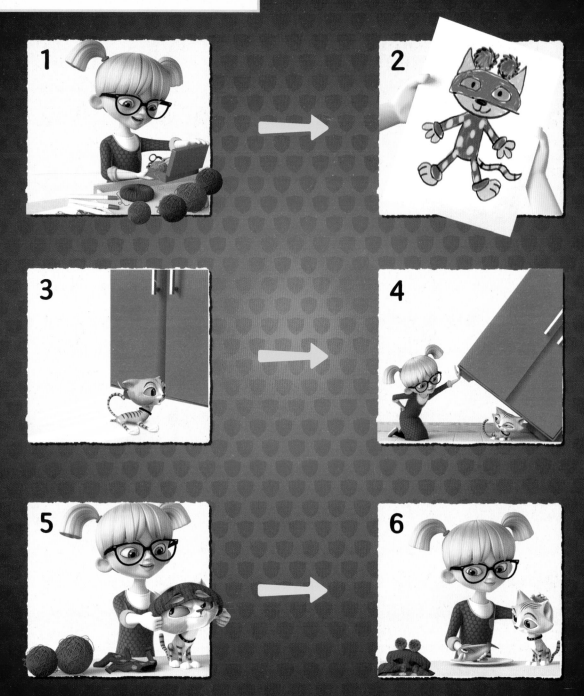